Crossing Laurel Run

Maxwell King

Coal Hill Review

For Louise Perkins King—
She taught me to love words.

Second Nature

The chief investment officer's papers
glide across the polished mahogany
high up here in the boardroom.
Thirty stories down, the spring surge
on the Allegheny River has taken her out of her banks,
flooding the walkway in front of the new stadium.
We take our seats around the table,
slipping comfortably across
the fine-grained leather of the mahogany chairs.
A line of young alders and maples,
planted three weeks ago in front of the ballpark,
has been swept away by the floodwaters.

First, the update on the portfolio:
everything is fine; we only lost a little
while all the indices indicate
that the others lost a lot.
Second, the timberland fund manager's report,
slid across the table to each of us
like an infield warm-up drill.
Just along the Seventh Street Bridge,
two large tree trunks have jammed
between the concrete walkway and the stone bridge pier,
creating an ad hoc dam that collects
branches, plastic bottles, assorted flotsam.

The investment officer has gone to the easel,
framed by the walnut paneling in the corner,
where he displays the latest U.S. Forest Service
North American Stumpage Report:

housing starts, board feet, stumpage—all up nicely.
At Seventh Street,
the river boils and surges
over the makeshift dam;
further out into the channel, the main current
hurtles along past the city
with all the dismissive force
of an ungovernable beast.

The CIO speaks of the regenerative power of the forest,
its faculty for yielding cash flow through the ages.

On Jennings Land

Along the Laurel Ridge, out of our pickup
       over to the fence
       above the Jennings cornfield—

a red-tailed hawk floats
       through the rising currents
       from the valley floor.

To the south, where the ridge flattens,
       we can see the outlines
       of our own land:

Thick green of the un-mowed field, pale thin lines
       of tedded hay,
       and that sad, spare beige of autumn

where the cornstalks wait to be cut.
       From this distance, the fields
       make an abstract mosaic—

no lines holding to the rectilinear notions
       we brought out
       here years ago;

all things tending, with a passage
       of time, toward the more
       promiscuous paths of the wild.

On Jennings land, tracks of goat and sheep
       arc and cross to the beck

of some atavistic impulse;

tangles of bull grass, multi-flora rose
and Japanese knotweed surge
from field to wood.

Doe Season

A spattering of frozen
blood in the snow—
granulated red pebbles—
tracks the right side
of the wounded deer's path;
at the barbed wire,
a wide, flinging arc
of blood pebbles,
tufts of brown fur
stuck to the fence.

Down a gully just
off White Oak Run, my wife
and I find a pool of red
and a pile of blue guts,
still steaming in the December air.
Across the creek,
in the woods
along Powdermill Ridge,
we can see two fawns
moving slowly

through the naked trees.
That evening, we take
a beef pot roast out
of its plastic, arrange
it in a pan with carrots
and onions and potatoes,

ready for the oven.
Then sit silently together
at the kitchen table,
fiddling with our forks.

The Weather

Carol came late and arrived softly—
an evening rainstorm and just a little
bluster with the tops of the trees.
And yet, a thousand miles south
she thrust ashore with such bombast
that the bungalows floated
across a sheet of storm-churned water
and the birds were speechless in the teeth of the wind.
Next day down there,
the stink of the mussel flats
spoke powerfully of all that had been displaced:
dead fish, the carcass of a dog,
tires, a lawn mower,
the single severed wing of a gull
and row upon row of fresh kelp.
What is it about the sea
that stirs so savage to the sky?
And what in the arc of the land—
pine-needle hump of the Ozarks—
that gently scrubs the menace
from the belly of the storm as it scuds upland?
One tall, half-dead hickory came down here;
this morning, Carol's last drizzle
is quietly busy cleaning the black loam
from the upended ball of roots.

the road again

ridge top to ridge top
the valley holds
a brown haze that obscures
the ribbon of roadway
along the other side/
here the heat
has softened the macadam
to a dark sticky gray,
the wheels of the semis
making a hissing slurry-sound
as my pickup pulls
round into the passing lane

clicking across the dial
to find willie's raspy-craggy
voice telling me
"my hee-rows have always been cowboys"/
bankrupt hocked up full
to the federal government
willie's response—hold a series
of benefit concerts for farmers
facing foreclosure—is as american
as his sing-song sentiment
"don't you hold onto nothin' too long"

five hours down
five hours back
same trip every week/
ribbony ridges of the alleghenies
rich green forests

rolling farms of pennsylvania
smoothing into
the gentle hills of maryland/
sometimes it seems
america is just scenes
seen from a highway

ammonia smell
of the restroom
sweet salt greasiness
of the french fries
hills terraced and topped
for boxy tract ranchers
jesus saves if you can read this
you're following too
shopping centers rising like spaceships
out of black-asphalt lakes
zinn's diner hearty family
double bed a.c. $59
callbox 41 bridge may be icy
work zone falling rock
cabela's world's foremost outfitter/
good god america i love you
your greed your waste
your hurry and impatience
none of these
obscure the rawboned beauty
of your energy your great
god-begotten gusto
for every inch of life

pushing you forward
without a fear without a thought

three fat guys in a cadillac
inches off my ass
caddy's broad chrome grin
looming in my rear-view mirror/
the semi grinding uphill
in second gear in front of me
pulls half into the breakdown and i follow/
caddy roaring by
fat guys laughing open-mouthed
cigar smoke pouring
from a quarter-open front window

trucker in a sleeveless tee
arms ropey with veins mottled with tattoos
hair sticking out in tufts
from under his red ball cap
leaning against the cab
of his semi at the pump
complaining bitterly to his cell phone
"i can't fuckin' get to delaware today
and that means i can't make providence
tomorrow—don't you fuckin' get it?
by the time i drop both loads
it won't even cover the diesel"

Near the Rock

The birds have retreated half a mile
on either side of the massive highway
built to track the coast—sparrows, robins, wrens,
even the sandpipers and gulls—fleeing
the awful racket and stink
of a ceaseless stream of cars and trucks
flowing south from Boston.

Back then, the fishermen made jokes
of the closeness of cod to God,
and some found a spiritual chord
in the beauty of the great silvery fish.

Today, looking out from Plymouth Harbor
through a sticky brown haze,
the thick air obscures
the shape of the cape
they named for their fish.
The trawling fleet sits at anchor
inside the jetty; not enough cod
left on the banks
to make the trip worth the diesel.

And they wrote letters home
to their brothers and sisters:
The fish are so many
we may walk on their backs
from shoal to shoal
and pluck the fattest for supper.

Catcher on the Bay

I patrol the half-moon beaches
of Monk Isle, walking against
a late-September wind coming
hard from the southwest.
These beaches are wind and tide-scalloped;
a series of mile-long ellipticals
that finish at each end
in sharp sandy points jutting into the bay.
I share them with horseshoe crabs
and a flock of gray gulls that keeps up
a constant hectoring chatter.
No people walk the tideline
with me in this late season,
and most often there are
no other boats besides mine
pulled up into the eel grass.

Conch shells are scattered
every few hundred feet along the sand,
many of them broken and empty;
a few still occupied by the meaty,
black, slug-like bodies of the conch.
Some of these are half eaten by gulls,
but a few are still whole and alive,
stranded in the bright sun by the tide.
I catch them up and hurl them
back into the cool, blue water.

Leaning over to inspect a shell,
I feel a sharp stab in my calf

and turn to find a bottle-green horsefly
biting me. I smack him with my palm
and he drops to the beach—one wing broken—
whirring around in an arc
that makes a perfect circle in the sand.

In the Bay

The wind and rain
come hard across the port bow,
the clatter of raindrops on the cabin roof
enough to drown the hum of the motor.
On my nod, the boatman
idles the engine and angles the bow
into the face of the wind.

My mother's fingers are tight, white
around the tin box.
We go to the stern together,
the others watching,
and tip the box down to the water.
The white-cap chop and rolling deck
make an awkward ballet of our endeavor.

Half the ashes are in the bay
when the boat comes off the wind
and a gust whips about the stern.
My father is on the water . . .
and on my hands and
across the front of my raincoat,
around the sleeves of my mother's sweater,
and in her hair.
She smiles a lovely, almost regal,
slightly wry, what-can-you-expect-from-life-anyway
smile for all of us,
and we close the lid to the box.

Elegy for Ingrid

These are not volunteers,

    these bright, gay sentinels
    lining the grassy bank
    above a mud-clotted barnyard.

They were stationed here
by a hand as delicate
and powerful as flowers;

their thin and reedy grace—

    swaying in the wind
    off the high pasture—

matched by a fierce resilience
that thrust their beauty
through the frost-hoary shale
and clay by the bank-barn.

It is here,

    in the path of late-afternoon
    sunlight washing down the bank,
    that we must spread
    her ashes.

Meridian Procession

Bright and sunny, bitter cold
and still in the valley. I persuade her
to leave the Sunday Times, the fireplace,
to go to the ridge. We follow Powdermill Trail
to the top, frozen branches tinkling in a light breeze,
bits of ice falling into our ski tracks—
looking down the valley
to a juddering wisp of smoke from our own chimney.

Later, we climb that other hill,
kissing and laughing and sweating,
throwing the quilt off the bed; rocking
so we almost come apart—
then hard together,
holding on and breathless.

In the evening, we take the farm road
behind the barn, truck tires crunching
in the rutted ice, up to wood's edge.
Motor off, doors open to a flood
of yellow light from a full moon.
The dog sits in the pickup bed,
nose up, nostrils flared, listening
to coyotes howling up the valley.

Talking Trees

I stop here always, dropping my bike
in the bed of brown needles, sitting
on my haunches between the ruts,
listening . . . the wind through
the tops of the lodge-pole pines,
a few high branches giving
voice in off-pitch creak. Two old
lower limbs groan against each other.
A faint rhythm of trunks bending and
bowing keeps the air alive; here and
there a patch of sun escapes
the canopy, fluttering to the forest floor.

The smell of pitch
carries the sweet sadness of remembrance,
and something of hope—
the times she and I stopped
here together; the power of the woods
to draw her here again. I feel
these trees need a listener;
it's that, and the resinous smell,
that bring me back.

Safe Haven

My mother cancels her dentist appointment, pulls the faded
   green tarp
out of the garage into the living room, sets it up like a tent
in front of the red brick fireplace. She takes a hot bath—
her small, wizened frame adrift in the big claw-footed tub—
and pours the first of her usual two late-afternoon glasses
   of sherry,
this time accompanied by 73 sleeping pills.
Then, already growing woozy, she
crawls into the tarp tent, checks to make sure the pilot light is out
on the gas logs, and turns the valve.

Later, from her hospital bed, she explains to me the logic—
at 88 and failing in eye and ear—of scheduling suicide ahead
of having her teeth fixed. And I explain to her about
the safety valve on the gas fire and how
they've made sleeping pills less deadly.
But I understand her logic so much better
than she understands the progress of safety.

Next week, sleepless through a long night,
I get up at 4:30 and walk the harbor road
between her house and mine, wondering how soon this soft, thin
   light
will slip over the sill into my mother's blue-wallpapered bedroom.
And when she rises to let out the dog, how will she greet the day?
The dog will apply the pragmatic approach that marks his every
   morning,
deliberate and business-like on the lawn. But my mother will
   wince—her

almost-sightless eyes feeling the light as pain—and turn from the
  window.

And then, how soon will she begin again
her gritty, high-plains trek to the nothing she is seeking?

Crossing Laurel Run

Climbing the arc
of the high-pasture hill
in six inches of new wet snow,
we track through a stubble
of the season's last cut of hay,
our boot prints puddling
with dark water.
Two old oaks are down
with ice in the branches;
as we cross Laurel Run
we hear a cracking and turn back
to see a towering poplar
fall dead with the weight.

In the evening,
together by the wood stove,
we sit in silence.
I stare at the page number
in my book; your needles
tick for a moment, then fall still.
I watch your face:
eyes closing, high cheeks
darkening with some thought
not shared to me.
I could tell you what I've lost;
that it is the same
as what you've lost.
And then we would fight again—
our struggle to move past
the truth, to find a way

to lend the greater weight to hope.

I put a hand on your arm;
you put a hand on my hand.
Isn't there something we might understand,
something we could know
in order to know what to say to each other?
You would say there is nothing to say.
For me, there is this,
perhaps only this:
the ice will come soon enough,
and we must try, until then,
to hold each other
in the incandescence of our own arc.

Stone Comfort

The glass panes in the French doors
are so perfectly clean I can see
each petal of the zinnias across
the terrace.

    Cream-colored paint
on the mullions, rose
and green of the Persian rug,

    dark sheen
(polished to a glowing shadow)
of the mahogany chairs.

    Do you want my love?
Do you want anything of us?

    Or just to sit
in the early morning sun,

        drinking Barry's tea, eating
        toast with English marmalade.

The Coming Cold

Carpet of yellow dandelion spreading
across the lower pasture to green clover
and meadow grass by the fence
along Powdermill Run. Cumulus
below a high cirrus haze, opening to let
spring sunshine flow across the fields
to Laurel Mountain twelve miles distant.
The smell of baking bread, commingled
with chords of Copeland's Appalachian Spring,
wafting through the kitchen window to the front porch.

I'm alive, sitting on an old wicker chair
in the thinning late-afternoon sunlight,
attended by the sorrowful voice of the oboe.

When I landed on the floor,
they knew right away
I was in trouble, tearing off my shirt,
pumping hard on my chest, blowing air into my mouth,
using their ingenious device
to send an arc of electricity from one side
of my chest, my heart, to the other.

The dog and I hike to the top
of the long hill behind the barn,
strong and steady on our pace.
We won't do this forever, or even
for long. But I will live on in the memory of the dog,
or she in mine. In just four months
it will be autumn again, a full year—

sunlight going cold on the floor of the porch,
meadow grass flattening with first frost,
snakes and varmints burrowing deep
against the coming cold.

High above
the lower pasture,
a red-tailed hawk shrieks
a warning to any
who would intrude
on her killing ground.